Law Firm Accounting

Steven M. Bragg

AccountingTools®

For more information about AccountingTools® products, visit our Web site at www.accountingtools.com.

Table of Contents

About the Author

Steven Bragg, CPA, has been the chief financial officer or controller of four companies, as well as a consulting manager at Ernst & Young. He received a master's degree in finance from Bentley College, an MBA from Babson College, and a Bachelor's degree in Economics from the University of Maine. He has been a two-time president of the Colorado Mountain Club, and is an avid alpine skier, mountain biker, and certified master diver. Mr. Bragg resides in Centennial, Colorado. He has written more than 300 books and courses, including *New Controller Guidebook*, *GAAP Guidebook*, and *Payroll Management*. He has also written *The Auditors* science fiction trilogy.

Steven maintains the accountingtools.com web site, which contains continuing professional education courses, the Accounting Best Practices podcast, and thousands of articles on accounting subjects.

Buy Additional AccountingTools Courses

AccountingTools offers more than 1,500 hours of CPE courses, with concentrations in accounting, auditing, finance, taxation, and ethics. Related courses that you might like include:

- Better Business Writing
- Effective Time Management
- Partnership Accounting
- Partnership Tax Guide
- Records Management

Go to accountingtools.com/cpe to view these additional courses.

AccountingTools®

Chapter 1
The Essentials of Law Firm Accounting

Introduction

A law firm needs accurate, up-to-date financial reports, so that its partners can easily understand the financial performance and financial position of the firm. Partners need this information to make decisions about ongoing operational and financial adjustments to the firm, as well as the likely amount of distributable income. In this chapter, we cover the essentials of law firm accounting – the financial statements used, how business transactions are compiled, the need for charge codes, and the specific aspects of certain revenue, expense, asset, and liability accounts.

Law Firm Financial Statements

A law firm should develop a standard set of financial statements that is designed to reveal the following aspects of the business:

- *Results*. The statement of revenues and expenses contains the aggregate amount of revenues and offsetting expenses for a reporting period, which nets to the firm's profit or loss. Many partners consider this to be the most important financial statement, since it is a strong indicator of financial performance.
- *Position*. The statement of net assets contains the assets, liabilities, and partner equity of the firm as of any point in time. This information can be used as an indicator of the liquidity of the business, where there needs to be enough assets on hand to pay for liabilities as they become due for payment.
- *Cash*. Ultimately, the only thing that matters from a financial perspective is the amount of cash that a firm is generating. The statement of cash flows reveals the amount of cash inflows and outflows related to operating, financial, and investing activities. Though this statement tends to be the least-read of the financial statements, a close examination of it, especially when it is presented over multiple reporting periods, can provide clues about the underlying health of the business.

The layout of these financial statements is described in detail in the following chapter.

The Flow of Transactions

The information in the financial statements comes from a summary of every business transaction, which is the general ledger. A business transaction is an economic event with a third party, which is measurable in money. Examples of business transactions are buying insurance from an insurer, paying wages to employees, and paying rent to the owner of a law office. The general ledger is the master set of accounts that summarizes all transactions occurring within the firm. When there are many transactions, as may be the case when paying many employees or when there are large numbers of billings to clients, these transactions may be offloaded into a subsidiary ledger, such as the payroll ledger or the billing ledger. Information in these subsidiary ledgers is summarized and posted to the general ledger. Posting is the process of shifting the balance in a subsidiary ledger into the general ledger. Once all business transactions have been summarized into the general ledger, the ending balances in the general ledger accounts are used to construct the financial statements.

This flow of information does not result in a set of financial statements that will have the same outcome, no matter who compiles the information. Instead, the statements contain some estimates regarding business transactions that may not be finalized for several months, and which are based on varying perceptions of the eventual outcome. For example, a law firm could set up an allowance for doubtful accounts that is an estimate of how many client billings will not be paid – the accuracy of this allowance will not be apparent for several months, after all client payments have been received.

Cash Basis and Accrual Basis Accounting

The cash basis of accounting is the practice of only recording revenue when cash has been received from a client, and recording expenses only when cash has been paid out. The cash basis is commonly used by smaller law firms. An alternative method for recording transactions is the accrual basis of accounting, under which revenue is recorded when earned and expenses are recorded when liabilities are incurred or assets consumed, irrespective of any inflows or outflows of cash. The accrual basis is most commonly used by larger law firms. A smaller firm will frequently begin keeping its books under the cash basis and then switch to the accrual basis when it has grown to a sufficient size.

> **Note:** Accounting software can be configured to work under either the cash basis or the accrual basis of accounting, usually by setting a flag in a setup table.

The cash basis of accounting has the following advantages:

- *Ease of use*. A person requires a reduced knowledge of accounting to keep records under the cash basis.
- *Taxation*. The method is commonly used to record financial results for tax purposes, since a firm can accelerate some payments in order to reduce its taxable profits, thereby deferring its tax liability.

However, the cash basis of accounting also suffers from the following problems:

- *Accuracy*. The cash basis yields less accurate results than the accrual basis, since the timing of cash flows does not necessarily reflect the proper timing of changes in the financial condition of a firm.
- *Manipulation*. A firm can alter its reported results by not cashing received checks or altering the payment timing for its liabilities.
- *Lending*. Lenders do not feel that the cash basis generates overly accurate financial statements, and so may refuse to lend money to a firm that is reporting under the cash basis.
- *Audited financial statements*. Auditors will not audit financial statements that were compiled under the cash basis of accounting, so a firm will need to convert to the accrual basis if it wants to have audited financial statements.
- *Management reporting*. Since the results of cash basis financial statements can be inaccurate, management reports should not be issued that are based upon it.

The main advantage of the accrual basis of accounting is that financial statements tend to better reflect actual circumstances, since revenues and their associated expenses are paired within the same period. This gives the reader a better understanding of actual financial performance in each reporting period.

The main disadvantage of the accrual basis is the need to include estimates in the financial statements to record transactions that have not been completed, or for which the associated paperwork has not yet been received. There are many rules associated with the creation of these estimates, which means that a significantly greater knowledge of accounting is needed to employ the accrual basis of accounting.

Many law firms prefer to use the cash basis, since it is simpler to use. To avoid the problems with inaccurate reporting that can occur under the cash basis, law firms may elect to use modified cash basis accounting, which contains some aspects of the accrual basis of accounting. It involves adding the following adjustments to cash basis accounting:

- Capitalize and depreciate fixed assets
- Record client disbursements receivable
- Record insurance premiums paid in advance
- Record loans payable
- Record retirement plan contributions payable

These changes do not entirely shift a firm's method of accounting all the way to the accrual basis, since the modified basis does not involve the following additional adjustments that are used under the accrual basis:

- Estimate the value of unbilled time
- Record accounts payable
- Record accrued expenses
- Record billed fees receivable

The exact amounts included in or excluded from cash basis accounting in order to arrive at a modified basis of accounting will vary by firm, since there are no accounting standards that address the specifics of this approach.

Accounting Terminology

A few specialized accounting terms will be used later in this text, so the following definitions are included to provide clarity in regard to how they are used:

- *Debits and credits*. When recording a business transaction, we record numbers in two accounts, where the debit column is on the left and the credit column is on the right. A *debit* is an accounting entry that either increases an asset or expense account, or decreases a liability or equity account. A credit is an accounting entry that either increases a liability or equity account, or decreases an asset or expense account.
- *Accruals*. An accrual allows a law firm to record expenses and revenues for which it expects to expend cash or receive cash, respectively, in a future reporting period. Using accruals allows a business to more closely adhere to the matching principle, where revenues and related expenses are recognized together in the same period. For example, an accrual can be recorded to recognize revenue before a billing is issued to a client.
- *Contra accounts*. A contra account offsets the balance in another, related account with which it is paired. If the related account is an asset account (which is usually the case), then a contra asset account is used to offset it with a credit balance. A law firm is most likely to use contra accounts to accumulate the depreciation that offsets its fixed assets, and to accumulate an allowance for doubtful accounts that offsets its fees receivable.
- *Reserves*. A reserve is an amount that is set aside for expected losses. For a law firm, reserves are most likely to be used in relation to client billings. A reserve is also called an allowance.

Fee Revenue

The essential source of revenue for a law firm is from the fees it charges. It does so by having its attorneys and administrative staff record their billable hours, which are then translated into billings, which are then paid by clients. The timing of when this revenue is recorded will vary, depending on whether the modified cash basis or accrual basis of accounting is used. Under the modified cash basis, the firm waits until clients pay for these billings before it recognizes any revenue. Under the accrual basis, the firm recognizes revenue at the end of the reporting period based on the hours that have been internally billed to clients, even if no billings have yet been issued. The essential difference between these two methodologies from a revenue perspective is that revenue is recognized sooner under the accrual basis – perhaps several months sooner – than would be the case under the modified cash basis.

EXAMPLE

Xavier, Yates and Zachary (XYZ) has installed a new billing system that requires its attorneys and administrative staff to enter their hours worked into a central timekeeping repository, which is then used to compile billings to clients. In its first month of operation (January), the system reports that all associates, in aggregate, billed $620,000 to clients. Of this amount, $500,000 was actually billed to clients, with the remaining $120,000 being held back for billing in later periods. None of the clients paid the billed amounts in January. Based on this scenario, if XYZ were using the modified cash basis of accounting, it would recognize no revenue in January based on the hours billed in that month (though it would recognize revenue from prior months for any cash received related to those months). If XYZ were to instead use the accrual basis of accounting, it would recognize the $500,000 of billings as revenue in January, as well as the $120,000 of unbilled revenue.

In the following sub-sections, we note a number of additional issues related to fee revenue.

Charge Codes

At the most simplified level of record keeping, a person would charge billable time to a client based on an assigned code that is unique to the client, so that one can then match revenues to costs for each client, to determine client-level profitability. Thus, a charge code could be as simple as:

	Charge Code
Smith Ironworks	3150

However, what if there are four different ongoing matters being handled for a client? Then the charge code needs to include extra digits to uniquely identify each matter. For example:

	Charge Code
Smith Ironworks – Form 8-K reviews	3150-001
Smith Ironworks – Initial public offering	3150-002
Smith Ironworks – Secondary offering	3150-003

This more complex coding structure allows for one to calculate profitability at the level of each individual matter for a client, while also allowing for the aggregation of revenues and expenses at the client level, to determine profits in total for each individual client.

The coding situation can be even more complex if the firm is organized into practice groups, since the partners may want to see profits aggregated at the practice group level. In the following example, the practice group code is inserted at the front of the charge code, since it represents the highest level of aggregation:

	Charge Code
Securities Law – Smith Ironworks – Form 8-K reviews	01-3150-001
Securities Law – Smith Ironworks – Initial public offering	01-3150-002
Securities Law – Smith Ironworks – Secondary offering	01-3150-003

An alternative arrangement is to track hours and costs using the coding contained within the Litigation Code Set, which is a standardized format that provides clients with consistent cost information by litigation task. The Code Set is designed to cover all contested matters, such as judicial litigation, binding arbitration, and regulatory/administrative proceedings. The Code Set appears in the following table.

Litigation Code Set

L100 – Case Assessment, Development and Administration	
L110	Fact Investigation/Development – Those actions taken to investigate the facts of a matter.
L120	Analysis/Strategy – The planning for a case, including legal research.
L130	Experts/Consultants – Locating and interviewing experts and consultants.
L140	Document/File Management – The creation and population of document and other databases.
L150	Budgeting – The development and revision of a matter.
L160	Settlement/Non-Binding ADR – Those activities involved in reaching a settlement, including the planning for and participation in settlement discussions.
L190	Other Case Assessment, Development and Administration – Those time charges not attributable to any other task.
L200 – Pre-Trial Pleadings and Motions	
L210	Pleadings – The development and review of complaints, answers, and counter-claims.
L220	Preliminary Injunctions/Provisional Remedies – The development of strategy for remedies, preparing motions and related tasks, attending court hearings, preparing witnesses, and related activities.
L230	Court Mandated Conferences – The preparation for and attendance at hearings and conferences, not including settlement conferences.
L240	Dispositive Motions – The development of strategies and papers related to summary judgment, as well as preparing for and attending related hearings.
L250	Other Written Motions and Submissions – Activities related to all other motions.
L260	Class Action Certification and Notice – Those activities related to class action litigation and related suits.

L300 – Discovery

L310   Written discovery – Activities related to interrogatories and requests to admit.

L320   Document production – Activities related to document requests, and sessions to resolve objections.

L330   Depositions – Activities related to depositions, including the identification of deponents, the timing of depositions, communicating with opposing counsel, preparing witnesses, attending depositions, and similar activities.

L340   Expert Discovery – The same as L330, except for expert witnesses.

L350   Discovery Motions – Activities related to the motions arising from the discovery process.

L390   Other Discovery – Activities related to other forms of discovery, such as medical examinations.

L400 – Trial Preparation and Trial

L410   Fact Witnesses – The preparation of non-expert witnesses for examination and cross-examination.

L420   Expert Witnesses – The preparation of expert witnesses for examination and cross-examination.

L430   Written Motions and Submissions – Activities related to written motions, both before and during trial, as well as trial briefs, jury instructions, and witness lists.

L440   Other Trial Preparation and Support – All other activities related to the preparation for and support of a trial.

L450   Trial and Hearing Attendance – Appearances at hearings, court-mandated conferences, and at trial.

L460   Post-Trial Motions and Submissions – Activities related to post-verdict matters in the trial court.

L470   Enforcement – Those activities related to the enforcement and collection of judgments or to the defense of those judgments.

L500 – Appeal

L510   Appellate Motions and Submissions – Activities related to motions and other filings before a reviewing body.

L520   Appellate Briefs – The preparation and review of appellate briefs.

L530   Oral Argument – Activities related to arguing an appeal before a reviewing body.

E100 – Expenses

E101   Copying

E102   Outside Printing

E103   Word Processing

E104   Facsimile

E105   Telephone

E106   Online Research

E107   Delivery Services/Messengers

E108	Postage
E109	Local Travel
E110	Out-of-Town Travel
E111	Meals
E112	Court Fees
E113	Subpoena Fees
E114	Witness Fees
E115	Deposition Transcripts
E116	Trial Transcripts
E117	Trial Exhibits
E118	Litigation Support Vendors
E119	Experts
E120	Private Investigators
E121	Arbitrators/Mediators
E122	Local Counsel
E123	Other Professionals
E124	Other

The coding for practice groups can be extensive, since there are many possible practice groups that may be formed within a larger law firm, as noted in the following exhibit.

Sample Practice Groups

Admiralty & maritime law	Elder law	Legal malpractice law
Antitrust law	Employee benefits law	Mass tort litigation
Appellate practice	Entertainment law	Mergers & acquisitions
Arbitration	Family law	Municipal law
Bankruptcy law	Franchise law	Nonprofit law
Civil rights law	Gaming law	Patent law
Commercial litigation	Health care law	Personal injury litigation
Construction law	Immigration law	Product liability litigation
Copyright law	International arbitration	Securities law
Criminal defense	Labor law	Tax law

The coding situation can be even more complex if the partners want to track profitability by individual office, which may call for yet another expansion of the charge code. While each of these charge code expansions has a logical basis, the underlying problem is that they eventually become unwieldy, resulting in a significant number of data entry errors that result in incorrect billings to clients, or at least a significant amount of labor to cross-check all hours charged before they are assembled into billings. Thus, one must balance reporting requirements against data accuracy when creating a system of charge codes.

Billing Calculations

The creation of client billings is not as simple as multiplying the hours worked for a person by that individual's standard hourly rate. Instead, one must consider several additional factors, such as:

- Overtime worked
- The efficiency of those conducting the work
- The value of the services provided

The result may be a billing amount that exceeds the standard rate that would normally be charged, or (more likely) the billing is for a lesser amount. If the billing exceeds the standard rate, the difference is called *over-realization*. If the billing is less than the standard rate, the difference is called *under-realization*. Because of the special nature of the billing process in a law firm, these billings must be examined by the partner responsible for a client before the billing is issued.

EXAMPLE

David Yates, partner at Xavier, Yates and Zachary, is examining the firm's labor records for the past month for a client, Billabong Machining Company. The hours charged and the associated standard billing rates are as follows:

Position	Hours Charged	Standard Rate	Extended Amount
Partner	12	$500	$6,000
Attorney	90	300	27,000
Administrative	20	65	1,300
			$34,300

Mr. Yates knows that the attorney assigned to this client was not especially efficient in conducting some of the work, and also realizes that the client is quite sensitive to perceived cases of overbilling. Consequently, he decides to reduce the total amount of the billing to $29,500. When compared to the standard amount of the billing, this results in under-realization of $4,800.

A new issue is that some legal work may be completed by generative artificial intelligence systems. If so, there is no longer an association between the hours worked by teams of attorneys and the amounts billed to clients. In these cases, it may make sense for a law firm to charge a flat fee for work completed by an AI, or perhaps charge a technology fee for the firm's use of the AI technology.

Timing of Billings

A law firm can engage in a variety of billing arrangements that can shift some client payments forward in time, roughly match hours expended with payments, or shift payments to the end of a task. The cash flow issues and accounting concerns with these approaches are as follows:

- *Retainers*. A law firm may request that its clients pay in advance for services that will be provided at a later date. If the firm is using the modified cash basis of accounting, these retainers are recognized as revenue upon receipt of the cash, even though no services have yet been performed. If the firm is using the accrual basis of accounting, retainers are recognized as a liability upon receipt of the cash, and are recognized as revenue only after the associated work has been performed. The advantage of a retainer, of course, is that the firm has no cash flow issues, since it already has the cash and has not yet made any offsetting expenditures.
- *Progress billings*. The most common arrangement is for billable hours to be compiled into a monthly billing and issued to clients immediately after month-end. Under the modified cash basis of accounting, these billings are not recognized as revenue until payment is received. Under the accrual basis, revenue is recognized as soon as the billing is issued. Progress billings are a reasonable approach from a cash flow perspective, since cash is typically received within one or two months of the related expenditures.
- *Single billing at end of work*. Some clients may request that they be billed just once, at the end of work for a specific task. Under the modified cash basis of accounting, these billings are not recognized as revenue until payment is received. Since a billing may not be issued until several months after the start of work, this can represent a substantial delay in revenue recognition. Under the accrual basis, revenue is recognized over the course of the work, as billable hours are completed. Single billing arrangements are not acceptable from a cash flow perspective, since payments may not be received until months after the related costs have been incurred.

When it is time to issue billings, a law firm should issue them as promptly as possible, since it is easier to collect them when clients have just experienced the benefits of the work provided. Ideally, partners should block out time in their calendars at the beginning of each month to contact clients and discuss the prior month's billings with them prior to the issuance of invoices, which greatly improves the rapidity of payment.

EXAMPLE

Xavier, Yates and Zachary (XYZ) uses the modified cash basis of accounting. It receives a $5,000 retainer from a client, for which it records the following entry:

	Debit	Credit
Cash [asset account]	5,000	
Professional fees [revenue account]		5,000

XYZ issues an $8,000 progress billing to a client in January. The firm receives payment from the client in March, at which time the following entry is recorded:

	Debit	Credit
Cash [asset account]	8,000	
Professional fees [revenue account]		8,000

XYZ begins work for a client in January and completes its efforts in April, after which it issues a $12,000 billing to the client. The firm receives payment from the client in June, at which time the following entry is recorded:

	Debit	Credit
Cash [asset account]	12,000	
Professional fees [revenue account]		12,000

EXAMPLE

Urchin, Verge and Wheaton (UVW) uses the accrual basis of accounting. It receives a $10,000 retainer from a client, for which it records the following entry:

	Debit	Credit
Cash [asset account]	10,000	
Unearned retainers [liability account]		10,000

UVW issues a $20,000 progress billing to a client in January, and immediately records the following entry:

	Debit	Credit
Fees receivable [asset account]	20,000	
Professional fees [revenue account]		20,000

The client pays UVW the $20,000 in March, which triggers the following entry:

	Debit	Credit
Cash [asset account]	20,000	
Fees receivable [asset account]		20,000

UVW begins work for a client in January and completes its efforts in May, after which it issues a $50,000 billing to the client. At the end of January, $14,000 of billable hours have been recorded against this project. Accordingly, the following entry is recorded at the end of January:

	Debit	Credit
Unbilled fees [asset account]	14,000	
Professional fees [revenue account]		14,000

UVW continues to accrue revenue in the following months, until it issues the $50,000 billing in May. The entry is:

	Debit	Credit
Fees receivable [asset account]	50,000	
Unbilled fees [asset account]		50,000

The client pays UVW in July, which triggers the following entry:

	Debit	Credit
Cash [asset account]	50,000	
Fees receivable [asset account]		50,000

Handling of Bad Debts

It is possible that a client will protest part of a billing, and so will only pay part of the total amount. In some cases, no payment will be forthcoming at all. The handling of these bad debts depends on whether a firm is using the modified cash basis of accounting or the accrual basis. If the modified cash basis is being used, the firm simply recognizes as revenue whatever amount is received, since revenue is only recognized at the point of cash receipt. If the firm is using the accrual basis, there are two options for how to proceed, which are:

- *Direct write-off.* The simplest approach is to write off each bad debt to a bad debt expense account, which also reduces the amount of professional fees recognized. However, bad debts tend to be recognized several months after revenue was already recognized (when billings were issued).

- *Allowance approach.* A more complex but theoretically correct approach is to set up an allowance for doubtful accounts when billings are issued and the associated revenue is recognized, so that the related bad debt expense is recognized right away, rather than on a delayed basis.

Both concepts are expanded upon in the following example.

EXAMPLE

Urchin, Verge and Wheaton (UVW) uses the accrual basis of accounting. As noted in the last example, it issued a $50,000 billing to a client in May. In July, the client pays $48,000 and refuses to pay the remaining $2,000. If UVW is using the direct write-off method, it records the following entry upon receipt of the cash:

	Debit	Credit
Cash [asset account]	48,000	
Bad debt expense [expense account]	2,000	
Fees receivable [asset account]		50,000

Under this approach, $50,000 of revenue is recognized in May and an offsetting $2,000 in July.

If UVW had instead used the allowance approach, it would have developed a standard bad debt percentage based on its historical experience with bad debts. This examination results in the finding that, on average, 4% of all billings are not paid. In May, UVW issues $1,000,000 of billings, which includes the $50,000 billing just described. As part of the month-end accounting activities, the firm recognizes 4% of the total billings in its allowance for doubtful accounts, using this entry:

	Debit	Credit
Bad debt expense [expense account]	40,000	
Allowance for doubtful accounts [contra asset account]		40,000

When UVW receives the $48,000 payment in July from its client and realizes that $2,000 is a bad debt, the resulting entry is:

	Debit	Credit
Cash [asset account]	48,000	
Allowance for doubtful accounts [contra asset account]	2,000	
Fees receivable [asset account]		50,000

Thus, the use of an allowance account allows for the immediate recognition of the likely bad debt expense in the same period when the related revenue is recognized, rather than on a delayed basis.

A likely issue with the use of the allowance account is that it is impossible to predict the amount of bad debts that will be incurred in the future with perfect precision. Thus, a firm will need to monitor the remaining size of the allowance for doubtful accounts on an ongoing basis, to see if it requires an additional adjustment, either to increase or reduce it.

Compensation Expenses

The accounting for payroll is an extensive accounting sub-discipline, for which the author's *Payroll Management* course provides an in-depth view of the mechanics of payroll processing. Beyond the general payroll processing issues, there are a few compensation topics that are specific to law firms, as noted in the following sub-sections.

Practice Group Designations

If personnel are permanently assigned to specific practice groups, it can make sense to link them in the payroll system to those practice groups. By doing so, the system can generate reports that specify the total compensation expense for each group. When paired with revenues, this information can yield most of the information needed to derive profits by practice group.

If personnel split their time between practice groups, it will be necessary to update practice group designations in the payroll system for each separate entry made into the timekeeping system. When this is the case, there is an increased risk that hours will be charged to the wrong practice groups.

Compensation Reporting

In order to attract and retain associates, partners need to understand the compensation levels of its attorneys, which is usually tracked based on the number of years since they graduated from law school. This information can then be compared to average compensation levels within the region, to see if any adjustments are needed to the pay structure of the firm. Such a report appears in the following exhibit.

Sample Compensation Reporting for Associates

Associate Year	Number of Associates	Total Compensation	Average Compensation
First	58	$7,250,000	$125,000
Second	46	5,853,500	127,250
Third	31	4,053,250	130,750
Fourth	23	3,142,375	136,625
Fifth	10	1,450,000	145,000
Sixth	6	912,000	152,000
Seventh	4	643,500	160,875
Eighth	3	506,250	168,750

The cost of the administrative staff can be substantial, so it can make sense to slice the cost of this group into as many segments as possible, to analyze whether the firm is incurring excessive costs. Here are several possibilities:

- Track the cost of time not charged to clients, by staff person
- Track the cost of any staff people not assigned to specific practice groups
- Identify compensation levels for staff people that significantly exceeds the median compensation for their position
- Compare administrative costs to revenue for each practice group on a trend line

Another analysis can focus on the costs of benefits consumed by employees, such as for health insurance, life insurance, pensions, and disability insurance. Possible analyses are:

- The multi-year trend for each classification of benefits, stated as the average amount per person
- Participation rates, noting how many employees are not taking advantage of each type of benefit
- Combine compensation and benefits information to derive the total compensation package for each individual

Reports should only be constructed and maintained if they contain actionable information. If the information in a report is no longer being used to make decisions, it is probably time to retire the report.

Operating Expenses

After compensation expenses, operating expenses are a significant part of the total cost structure of a law firm. Depending on how a firm is organized, it will probably want to track the following operating expenses:

- Business taxes
- Charitable contributions
- Cleaning services
- Depreciation of fixed assets
- Express delivery services
- Information technology costs
- Insurance (professional liability, general liability, etc.)
- Interest expense
- Library costs (books and reference materials)
- Occupancy taxes
- Office equipment rental costs
- Office rent
- Office supplies

- Professional services (accountants, actuaries, consultants, etc.)
- Repairs and maintenance
- Storage costs for records
- Telephone costs
- Uncollectible client disbursements
- Utilities

One way to control operating expenses is to construct a month-by-month budget for each expense, and then produce a budget-versus-actual report for each month. Any unusually large variances can then be investigated in depth. However, this report may not be very useful if the budget figures do not reflect reality.

Another possibility is to report on these expenses in a trailing 12-month format, so that the trend of actual expenses is clearly visible for the past year. This latter approach typically simplifies the task of spotting anomalies. The following exhibit shows how a trend line analysis can be constructed.

Sample Trend Line Expense Analysis

	Jan.	Feb	Mar.	Apr.	May	Jun.	Jul.	Aug.
Occupancy costs	$20,000	$20,000	$22,000	$22,000	$22,000	$22,000	$0	$44,000
Office supplies	2,400	2,100	2,300	2,500	2,000	4,000	1,500	2,200
Utilities	4,000	4,200	3,500	3,000	2,500	2,400	2,000	2,200

In the preceding exhibit, there is a clear bump-up in the monthly rent rate in March, as well as a missed rent invoice in July that was recorded in August, resulting in twice the normal occupancy cost in August. The office supplies expense varies somewhat around the low $2,000 range, except for a jump in the expense in June that may be worth additional investigation. Finally, the utilities expense is seasonal, showing increased heating costs during the winter months that gradually decline over time.

Yet another reporting option is to charge certain expenses to individual attorneys, such as telephone costs, professional services, express delivery services, and uncollectible client disbursements. If this approach is followed, be sure to couple the expense tracking with the revenues generated by attorneys, to ascertain profit levels by individual. When assigning costs to attorneys, be sure to limit cost assignments to those costs that are *direct costs*. These costs are ones that will only be incurred if the linked individual works for the firm. Thus, a car lease on behalf of an attorney should be linked to that individual, since the lease could be cancelled if he or she no longer worked for the firm. There are generally few direct costs in a law firm – most costs are general expenses that are needed to operate the entire organization.

Reimbursable Costs

Law firms incur costs on behalf of their clients to a much greater extent than in other industries, which means that a law firm needs a robust system for identifying and recording these costs by client, as well as to bill clients for reimbursement. Examples of the costs that are routinely incurred on behalf of clients are:

- Court costs
- Filing fees
- Travel expenses

When a law firm incurs these costs, it records them in the client disbursements receivable account, which is an asset account. When clients reimburse the firm, the payments offset the receivable. Thus, reimbursable costs are not recognized as revenue, nor is there any impact on the reported amount of profit or loss. The only exception is when a client refuses to reimburse the firm, in which case the unpaid amount is charged to expense.

The situation differs somewhat when a law firm is billing clients for costs it has incurred in-house, such as photocopying and secretarial support. It is possible to account for them in the manner just noted for costs incurred from third parties. However, it is also possible to account for them as expense reductions. If so, one can either pass the specific costs incurred to the client, or calculate the average cost of the service provided and then bill clients based on the number of units used by them. These concepts are expanded upon in the following example.

EXAMPLE

Urchin, Verge and Wheaton (UVW) incurs $5,000 of court costs and filing fees on behalf of a client, Armadillo Industries. The initial entry to record these costs is:

	Debit	Credit
Client disbursements receivable [asset account]	5,000	
Cash [asset account]		5,000

Upon receipt of the reimbursement payment from Armadillo, UVW records this entry:

	Debit	Credit
Cash [asset account]	5,000	
Client disbursements receivable [asset account]		5,000

UVW also incurs $7,500 of in-house costs working on behalf of Armadillo, for which the initial entry is:

	Debit	Credit
Photocopying expenses [expense account]	7,500	
Cash [asset account]		7,500

The accountant discusses how to account for these costs with the partner in charge of administration. One possibility is to include the specific cost incurred in the client billing, so that the billing results in a reduction of the expense on UVW's books. The entry would be:

	Debit	Credit
Client disbursements receivable [asset account]	7,500	
Photocopying expenses [expense account]		7,500

The accountant suggests another option, which is to calculate the average cost of photocopying for the firm during the month on a per-page basis, track the number of pages specifically attributable to Armadillo, and then charge the client based on this usage. In the past month, the firm photocopied 100,000 pages for its various clients. The total cost of photocopying within the month was $0.12 per page. The photocopies specifically created on behalf of Armadillo numbered 62,000. Therefore, the firm should bill Armadillo $7,440 based on its average billing rate for photocopying.

At the end of the preceding example, we noted that an average administrative rate should be derived for each month and then used as the basis for billings to clients. Actually, a more efficient approach is to estimate the average rate for a longer period, such as the preceding year or the last quarter, and apply that rate for an extended period of time. Doing so reduces the accounting labor associated with calculating the rate to be charged.

Distributable Income

From the perspective of a law firm partner, the essential financial statement line item is not its net income (calculated as revenues minus expenses), but rather the amount of distributable income. *Distributable income* is the amount of net income that is available for distribution to active partners. The amount of distributable income is usually less than the amount of net income, where the difference is the amount paid out to former partners in the firm. A firm may choose to break down these payments at the bottom of its income statement with the following line items:

+ Net income
- Payments to former partners
= Partners' distributable income

Payments to Former Partners

The amount of net income reported by a firm may be significantly reduced by the amount paid out to former partners. There are several types of former partners, such as:

- Partners who retired from the firm
- Partners who have left the firm for reasons other than retirement
- The estates of partners who have died

The amount of these payments is governed by the firm's partnership agreement, or from more specific agreements with individual partners. These amounts represent the share of former partners in the firm's net income. The amounts paid out to former partners may involve fixed periodic sums or a percentage of income, perhaps with a cap on the total amount paid out, depending on the terms of the underlying agreement.

> **Note:** When payments to former partners are not based on the amount of net income reported by a firm, they are stated within the expenses section of the income statement, and so are used to arrive at the net income figure.

Receivables

A law firm has three types of receivables. The most obvious is fee billings to clients, which are billable hours that have been formally assembled into an invoice and issued to a client. In addition, it has unbilled fees, which are hours charged to client matters, but which have not yet been billed. Finally, there are client disbursements receivable, which are costs incurred by the firm on behalf of clients, which have been billed to clients.

If a firm uses the accrual basis of accounting, then it should maintain two reserves related to receivables, which are:

- *Allowance for doubtful accounts.* This is a reserve against billings for which the firm never receives payment. When monthly billings are issued, an associated amount of bad debt expense is recognized, usually based on the firm's bad debt history. When actual bad debts are later uncovered, they are charged against this reserve. This is a standard reserve account in many industries.
- *Reserve for estimated unrealizable amounts.* A firm should recognize revenue for billable hours that have not yet been billed to clients. However, the partners may decide not to include some of these billed hours in the billings that are eventually issued, perhaps because they do not want to exceed a certain amount of billings with certain clients, or perhaps because they feel that the work was inefficiently performed. In these cases, a reserve is set aside for estimated unrealizable amounts. The amount in this reserve is periodically examined and adjusted, depending on the size of the unbilled amounts with which it is paired and the latest realization estimates. This reserve is unique to professional services firms.

Both reserves can be difficult to estimate, for reasons that are unique to the legal profession. For example, a client is less likely to pay the entire amount of a billing if its relationship with the firm is relatively weak, it is new to the relationship, or it is experiencing financial difficulties. Further, the reserve for estimated unrealizable amounts is more difficult to determine when the firm has a large proportion of new associates and paralegals, who are more likely to be inefficient.

A particular concern with overdue legal billings is that quite a high proportion of them become uncollectible once they are more than a few months old. Consequently, it makes sense for a law firm to establish a significantly larger allowance for bad debts as its uncollected receivables age. A good way to do this is to print the aged accounts receivable report (readily available as a standard report in most accounting software packages). This report aggregates unpaid billings into 30-day time buckets, such as 0-30 days old, 31-60 days old, and so forth. One can assign a progressively higher bad debt percentage to the older time buckets to arrive at a total estimate for the allowance for doubtful accounts. The concept is addressed in the following example.

EXAMPLE

Greene, Holbrook and Ignatius (GHI) has recently installed a new accounting software system that contains an aged accounts receivable report. As of the current date, the report shows the following totals:

Total	0-30 Days Old	31-60 Days Old	61-90 Days Old	90+ Days Old
$3,800,000	$2,100,000	$1,050,000	$510,000	$140,000

The partner in charge of administration realizes that this report can be used to develop an allowance for doubtful accounts, so she calculates an estimated bad debt percentage based on the time buckets in the report, using historical bad debt information. The result is the following enhanced report, which yields an estimated bad debt amount of $170,300.

	0-30 Days Old	31-60 Days Old	61-90 Days Old	90+ Days Old
Billings outstanding	$2,100,000	$1,050,000	$510,000	$140,000
Bad debt percentage	2%	5%	8%	25%
Estimated bad debt	$42,000	$52,500	$40,800	$35,000

Fixed Assets

A fixed asset is a purchased item that has a life span of greater than one reporting period, and which exceeds the firm's capitalization limit. The capitalization limit is the amount paid for an asset, above which it is recorded as a fixed asset. If an asset costs less than the capitalization limit, it is instead charged to expense as incurred.

A law firm is most likely to purchase fixed assets that fall within the following classifications:

- *Computer equipment.* Includes servers, network equipment, desktop computers, laptop computers, and printers.
- *Furniture and fixtures.* Includes desks, credenzas, bookcases, chairs, conference tables, and so forth.
- *Leasehold improvements.* Includes the construction costs needed to build out leased space.
- *Office equipment.* Includes photocopiers and similar equipment.

The costs incurred for fixed assets are usually assigned to one of the preceding accounts, in order to clarify where the firm is investing its funds. These designations are also useful for assigning different useful lives to fixed assets. For example, computer equipment may be expected to last three years, while the expectation may be five years for office equipment and seven years for furniture and fixtures. Leasehold improvements are expected to last for the lesser of the lease term or the useful life of the underlying asset.

Fixed assets are depreciated; depreciation is the planned, gradual reduction in the recorded value of a fixed asset over its useful life by charging it to expense. Law firms tend to use an accelerated depreciation method in order to recognize more expense in the early years of the life of an asset, thereby driving down reported income and deferring the related income taxes. The exception is leasehold improvements, for which the charge to expense is on a straight-line basis.

The status of a firm's fixed assets can be compiled into a summary schedule that notes the balances in all fixed asset accounts at the beginning of the year, changes to the accounts during the year, and the resulting ending balances. A sample presentation of this schedule appears in the following exhibit.

Sample Fixed Assets Schedule

	20X2 Beginning Balance	Additions	Retirements	20X2 Ending Balance
Fixed assets:				
Computer equipment	$182,000	$15,000	-$10,000	$187,000
Furniture & fixtures	310,000	37,000	-5,000	342,000
Leasehold improvements	287,000	--	--	287,000
Office equipment	58,000	20,000	-18,000	60,000
Totals	837,000	72,000	-33,000	876,000
Accumulated depreciation	-216,000	-18,000	33,000	-201,000
Fixed assets, net	$621,000	$54,000	$--	$675,000

Loan Liabilities

A law firm may obtain a bank loan, usually to pay for fixed assets or to provide it with sufficient working capital to maintain operations while waiting for clients to submit payments. To protect their loaned funds, banks may impose restrictions on a law firm. For example, a bank may require that partners maintain a certain amount of equity in the firm for the duration of the loan. Or, a bank may limit the amount of a loan to a percentage of the firm's fees receivable and unbilled fees. In both cases, the intent is to ensure that the firm has sufficient assets that the bank can access, in case it needs to recover the unpaid portion of a loan.

Partner Accounts

Each partner has a separate *capital account*. This is used by partnerships to track the net investment balance of the partners from the perspective of the firm. In essence, the capital account contains the transactions noted in the following table.

Capital Account Transactions

	Beginning balance in the capital account
+	Investments made by the partner
+	Subsequent profits of the partnership
-	Subsequent losses of the partnership
-	Subsequent draws paid to the partner
=	Ending balance in the capital account

The balance in a capital account is usually a credit balance, since this is an equity account, and all equity accounts have a natural credit balance. However, the amount of losses and draws can sometimes shift the account balance into debit territory. It is usually only possible for the account to have a debit balance if the firm has received debt funding to offset the loss of capital.

Profits and losses are not assigned to partner capital accounts on a continual basis. Instead, up to a year may pass before there is a *break period*, when these assignments are made. There may be more than one break period in a year (such as quarterly). However, each additional break period requires more work by the accountant to allocate profits and losses, so the number should be minimized unless there is a demonstrated benefit associated with more frequent assignments.

A major concern for a partner is the beginning balance in the capital account. Depending on the terms of the partnership agreement, the allocation of profits and losses to partner capital accounts is based on the *beginning* balance. Consequently, if a partner makes an investment in a partnership partway through the fiscal year, the amount of this investment may not be included in the calculation of profit and loss allocations – it depends on the terms of the partnership agreement.

The same issue relates to draws paid to a partner. Ideally, draws should be made after profits and losses have been allocated to partners. Otherwise, the amount of a draw even a few days before a break period might count as a reduction in the beginning balance of the capital account, which reduces the amount of profits or losses allocated to the partner. Again, the nature of this calculation depends on the terms of the partnership agreement.

The calculation of profit distributions among partners is based on the formula stated in the underlying partnership agreement – there is no standard approach. That being said, it is relatively common for law firms to allocate income based on a profit sharing percentage that varies based on the type of partner. For example, a newer partner may receive a smaller percentage of profits, while a larger percentage is awarded to partners who have been with the firm for a certain period of time. Depending on the underlying partnership agreement, there may also be a lesser percentage of profits awarded to retired partners. This concept is used in the following example.

EXAMPLE

Davis, Enderby and Fallows (DEF) has 20 partners, of which five are classified as junior partners, 12 as senior partners, and three as retired partners. The partnership agreement states that a junior partner receives 60% of the profits earned by a senior partner, while a retired partner earns 10% of the profits earned by a senior partner. The firm generated profits of $10 million in the past year. This results in the following profit-sharing allocation:

	Number of Partners	Per-Partner Allocation	Total Profit Allocation
Senior partners	12	$653,595	$7,843,140
Junior partners	5	392,157	1,960,785
Retired partners	3	65,359	196,075
	20		$10,000,000

Junior partners are typically required to make an investment in the firm. If they do not initially have sufficient capital to do so, they may be required to set aside a portion of their annual profit allocation, which increases their investment in the firm. Once their investment reaches the level designated in the partnership agreement, they can take the full amount of their profit allocations.

> **Note:** The need for partner accounts in a law firm gives rise to one of the most specialized accounting positions, the partners' accounts supervisor. This person is responsible for maintaining accurate accounting records for each partner's account, devising income allocation calculations that are in compliance with the underlying partnership agreement, and ongoing partner account reporting.

Interest on Lawyer Trust Accounts

When a law firm has control over the funds of a client, it is required to store these funds in a separate trust account, which is called an Interest on Lawyer Trust Accounts, or IOLTA. Under IOLTA rules, lawyers can place client funds in an interest-bearing trust account at a bank. The interest earned from this account is then forwarded to the applicable state IOLTA board, which uses these funds to finance a variety of activities, including the following:

- Civil legal services
- Enhancing justice administration
- Funding grants to nonprofit organizations
- Funding law school scholarships
- Legal aid for low-income residents

Every state has a separate IOLTA program. There are some differences in the rules used by each state; for example, IOLTA is mandatory in some states, and voluntary in others.

The accounting for an IOLTA account is fairly simple. For example, a law firm agrees to provide legal services to a local manufacturing company, representing it in a lawsuit. The company sends the law firm a $20,000 retainer, which the law firm's accountant deposits in the trust account. This results in the following entry:

	Debit	Credit
IOLTA account [asset account]	20,000	
Client trust liability [liability account]		20,000

The firm's attorneys then log 10 hours of their time on the client's case, at a rate of $250 per hour. This results in a billing of $2,500, which the accountant transfers from the IOLTA account to the firm's bank account, with the client's approval. This results in two entries, the first of which is to reverse $2,500 of the funds in the IOLTA account:

	Debit	Credit
Client trust liability [liability account]	2,500	
IOLTA account [asset account]		2,500

The next entry moves the $2,500 to the law firm's bank account and recognizes income in the amount of the billed hours.

	Debit	Credit
Law firm checking account [asset account]	2,500	
Income [income account]		2,500

You should maintain accurate records for all transfers into and out of an IOLTA account, no matter how small they may be, along with appropriate documentation that explains each one. This is especially important if your state bar wants to review these records.

> **Note:** You should maintain a separate ledger for each client, to keep track of the remaining amount being held in trust.

A key concern with IOLTA accounts is removing funds from them before the client has agreed to the transfer. These early removals may be considered borrowing from the account, which can lead to an ethics violation and even disbarment.

Summary

This chapter covered the core components of law firm accounting, including the basis of accounting, revenue calculations, charge codes, and the journal entries pertaining to various revenue and expense transactions. Much of the information covered here is recorded in the general ledger, from which the financial statements are constructed, as described in the next chapter.

Chapter 2
Law Firm Financial Statements

Introduction

As noted in the preceding chapter, many law firms choose to use the modified cash basis of accounting, which is midway between the cash basis and the accrual basis of accounting. In this chapter, we explore the structure of financial statements that are constructed under both the modified and accrual bases of accounting. The discussion includes examples of financial statement formats, as well as examples of the more common disclosures.

Statement of Net Assets

The statement of net assets aggregates a law firm's assets and liabilities into a small set of general categories, consistently applied over multiple periods. This statement also reports on the amount of partners' equity, which is the difference between the reported amounts of assets and liabilities. The statement reveals these amounts as of a specific point in time, such as the end of a month, quarter, or year. A sample statement follows.

Sample Statement of Net Assets

Xavier, Yates and Zachary
Statement of Net Assets
Modified Cash Basis of Accounting

	20X2
Current assets:	
Cash and cash equivalents	$1,600,000
Short-term investments	700,000
Client disbursements receivable	350,000
Advances and deposits	150,000
Prepaid insurance	200,000
Total current assets	3,000,000
Property and equipment	4,000,000
Less: Accumulated depreciation	1,500,000
Net property and equipment	2,500,000
Total assets	$5,500,000
Current liabilities:	
Accounts payable	$800,000
Employee payroll withholdings	150,000
Accrued retirement plan contributions	50,000
Total current liabilities	1,000,000
Long-term notes payable	2,000,000
Total liabilities	3,000,000
Net assets	$2,500,000
Net assets represented by:	
Partners' capital accounts	$1,500,000
Partners' current accounts	1,000,000
	$2,500,000

In the preceding statement, two line items are unique to law firms. One is the partners' capital accounts line item, which states the total amount of capital invested in the firm by its partners. The other line item is partners' current accounts, which states the total amount of earnings not yet distributed to the partners. These accounts can be combined for presentation purposes, though they are still tracked in the general ledger as separate accounts.

If a law firm is organized as a professional corporation, then the net assets section of the statement is replaced by a stockholders' equity section that breaks down equity into common stock (the par value of the shares issued), additional paid-in capital (the difference between par value and the amount received for each share) and retained earnings (the cumulative amount of profits that have not yet been paid out as dividends). For example:

Shareholders' equity:	
Common stock	$10,000
Additional paid-in capital	1,490,000
Retained earnings	1,000,000
	$2,500,000

If a firm instead chooses to use the accrual basis of accounting, the statement of net assets expands to include all types of receivables, unbilled hours worked, and a variety of accrued expenses, mostly related to liabilities that will be coming due within one year. Also, the name of the statement changes; it is now referred to as the balance sheet. A sample appears in the following exhibit (which is for a different sample firm).

Sample Balance Sheet

Urchin, Verge and Wheaton
Balance Sheet
Accrual Basis of Accounting

	20X2
Current assets:	
Cash and cash equivalents	$2,000,000
Short-term investments	4,500,000
Fees receivable	12,000,000
Unbilled fees	8,000,000
Client disbursements receivable	1,500,000
Advances and deposits	300,000
Prepaid insurance	200,000
Total current assets	28,500,000
Property and equipment	7,000,000
Less: Accumulated depreciation	2,500,000
Net property and equipment	4,500,000
Total assets	$33,000,000
Current liabilities:	
Accounts payable	$4,000,000
Employee payroll withholdings	400,000
Accrued retirement plan contributions	600,000
Other payables	250,000
Total current liabilities	5,250,000
Long-term notes payable	5,750,000
Total liabilities	11,000,000
Partners' equity:	
Partners' capital accounts	5,000,000
Partners' current accounts	17,000,000
Total partners' equity	22,000,000
Total liabilities and partners' equity	$33,000,000

Shifting to the accrual basis of accounting calls for new systems that can provide the new line items just stated for an accrual-basis balance sheet. These systems include:

- *Unbilled fees.* The firm needs a tracking system in which the staff records its hours worked, by client, from which unbilled hours can be pulled at the end of each reporting period.
- *Allowance for bad debts.* The firm needs a system for accruing an expense for invoiced amounts that have been billed, but which will not be collected. This amount can be based on the firm's prior experiences with bad debt losses, adjusted for specific knowledge about which clients are unlikely to pay.
- *Accrued expenses.* The firm should maintain schedules for recurring costs, so that it can determine those areas in which supplier invoices have not yet been received or for which payroll has not yet been run, but for which an expense must be recorded. For example, it may be necessary to formulate accruals for unpaid wages, rent, utilities, and pension payments at the end of each reporting period.

Statement of Revenues and Expenses

The statement of revenues and expenses aggregates a law firm's revenues and expenses into a small number of line items, consistently applied over multiple periods. This statement ends in a net income or net loss figure, from which a distributable income figure is derived. A sample statement follows.

Sample Statement of Revenues and Expenses

Xavier, Yates and Zachary
Statement of Revenues and Expenses
Modified Cash Basis of Accounting

	20X2
Revenues:	
Professional fees	$18,000,000
Other services	2,000,000
	20,000,000
Expenses:	
Employee compensation	7,000,000
Occupancy costs	2,500,000
Office expenses	1,200,000
Professional activities	800,000
General business expenses	500,000
Net income	12,000,000
Payments to former partners	2,000,000
Distributable income	$10,000,000

Statement of Changes in Partners' Accounts	
Partners' current accounts:	
Balance at beginning of year	800,000
Distributable income	10,000,000
Payments to active partners	-9,700,000
Transfers to capital accounts	-100,000
Balance at end of year	1,000,000
Partners' capital accounts:	
Balance at beginning of year	900,000
Capital contributions by partners	500,000
Capital withdrawals by partners	--
Transfers from current accounts	100,000
Balance at end of year	1,500,000
Total partners' accounts	$2,500,000

The preceding sample statement ended in a statement of changes in partners' equity during the period, separating out the activity during the reporting period in the firm's current and capital accounts.

In the preceding example, payments to former partners were categorized in a separate line item after the reported amount of net income. This is done in order to determine the profitability of the core operations of the firm before non-operating expenses.

If a law firm is organized as a professional corporation, then income taxes are paid by the corporation, rather than having this obligation flow through to the partners. Also, the Statement of Changes in Partners' Accounts is replaced by a Statement of Changes in Shareholders' Equity, which reveals any changes in the various equity accounts during the reporting period.

If a firm chooses to use the accrual basis of accounting, the format of the preceding statement of revenues and expenses is unchanged, though its title is altered to the "income statement" or "statement of income".

Statement of Cash Flows

The statement of cash flows presents the cash inflows and outflows experienced during a reporting period, with these flows further broken down into operating, investing, and financing activities. The types of cash flows found within each of these activities for a law firm are:

- *Cash flows from operating activities*. Includes receipts from billings, as well as payments for payroll, rent, and employee benefits.
- *Cash flows from investing activities*. Includes payments for the purchase or sale of fixed assets.
- *Cash flows from financing activities*. Includes the receipt of cash from loans, loan payments, payments made to former partners, and draws by current partners.

There are two acceptable modes of presentation for the statement of cash flows, which are the direct method and the indirect method. The direct method requires a firm to present cash flow information that is directly associated with the items triggering cash flows, such as:

- Cash collected from clients
- Interest and dividends received
- Cash paid to employees
- Cash paid to suppliers
- Interest paid

Few organizations collect information as required for the direct method, so they instead use the indirect method. Under the indirect approach, the statement begins with the net income or loss reported on the statement of revenues and expenses, and then makes a series of adjustments to this figure to arrive at the amount of net cash provided by operating activities. These adjustments typically include the following:

- Depreciation
- Provision for losses on receivables
- Gain or loss on sale of assets
- Change in receivables
- Change in payables

A sample statement using the indirect method of presentation appears in the following exhibit.

Sample Statement of Cash Flows

Addison, Bates, and Chesterton
Statement of Cash Flows
Modified Cash Basis of Accounting

	20X2
Cash flows from operating activities:	
Net income	$12,000,000
Reconciliation to net cash provided by operating activities	
Depreciation	80,000
Decrease in client disbursements receivable	120,000
Net change in other assets and liabilities	200,000
Net cash provided by operating activities	12,200,000
Cash flows from investing activities:	
Payments for property and equipment	-80,000
Proceeds from the sale of property and equipment	10,000
Purchase of investments	-300,000
Proceeds from the sale of investments	280,000
Net cash used in investing activities	-90,000
Cash flows from financing activities:	
Proceeds from bank loan	100,000
Capital withdrawals by partners	--
Draws by active partners	-9,700,000
Payments to former partners	-2,000,000
Capital contributions from partners	500,000
Net cash used in financing activities	-11,100,000
Net increase in cash and cash equivalents	
Cash and cash equivalents – beginning of year	3,990,000
Cash and cash equivalents – end of year	$5,000,000

If a law firm is organized as a professional corporation, then the treatment of payments to partners changes from the financing activities section of the report to the operating activities section.

If a firm chooses to use the accrual basis of accounting, the format and title of the statement of cash flows remains unchanged.

Notes to Financial Statements

In addition to the financial statements, it may be necessary to provide additional details, which are stated in the notes accompanying the statements. These notes are considered an integral part of the financial statements, so when one is referring to the financial statements as a whole, this includes the accompanying notes. The notes that accompany the financial statements will vary by law firm, but will usually include the following core disclosures:

- *Description of operations*. State the legal form of the business, the nature of the firm's practice, its client base, and the locations from which it operates. For example:

   XYZ provides international tax services, primarily to Fortune 500 companies around the world. The partnership operates from offices in New York, London, and Singapore.

- *Significant accounting policies*. State those key accounting policies that have a material impact on the derivation of net assets and/or net income. Clarifying these policies is especially important when the accounting policies differ from standard industry practice. The policies described usually cover revenue and expense recognition, depreciation, and the treatment of income taxes. For example:

   The partnership prepares its financial statements using the modified cash basis of accounting. This approach uses the cash basis of accounting, modified to include the capitalization of fixed assets and their subsequent depreciation, as well as the capitalization and subsequent amortization of prepaid insurance costs. This approach differs from the accrual basis of accounting in that revenues are recorded when cash is received, and expenses are recorded when paid, rather than when obligations are incurred.

   The partnership depreciates its fixed assets on the straight-line basis over periods ranging from three to ten years, depending on the nature of the assets. Leasehold improvements are amortized on a straight-line basis over the lesser of their estimated useful lives or the life of the associated property lease.

The partnership does not recognize a provision for income taxes, since the profits of the partnership are passed through to its partners, who are responsible for payment of these taxes.

- *Borrowing arrangements.* State the terms associated with any lending arrangements, including the amounts, interest rates, repayment terms, and reasons for the arrangements. For example:

  The partnership has obtained a five-year term loan from Columbine State Bank that allows the firm to borrow a maximum of $3,000,000 to finance various asset purchases. The interest rate on the loan is 2% over the bank's prime rate. The loan must be repaid in a single balloon payment on December 31, 20X7. Under the terms of this loan, the partnership cannot enter into any additional lending arrangements.

- *Lease obligations.* State the terms associated with any lease arrangements, which usually relate to office space and office equipment. The disclosure should include the minimum annual lease payments, in aggregate, in each of the next five years and thereafter. For example:

  The partnership has entered into several lease obligations related to its four office locations. The total rental expense related to these leases in the current year was $620,000. Minimum annual lease commitments in each of the next five years are as follows:

Year	
20X2	$640,000
20X3	480,000
20X4	480,000
20X5	240,000
20X6	240,000
Thereafter	600,000
	$2,680,000

- *Obligations to former partners.* State the nature of any agreements with former partners, where the partnership continues to make payments to them. For example:

  The partnership is obligated to make payments to its retired partners. The amounts paid depend on the retirement options selected by each individual partner, but are limited to 20% of the total partnership net income in each year. In the past year, the partnership paid approximately $2,000,000 to its retired partners.

- *Retirement plans.* State the nature of the retirement plan (a defined benefit plan[1] or a defined contribution plan[2]), who is covered by it, vesting requirements, and the funding status of the plan. For example:

  [For a defined benefit plan] The partnership operates a defined benefit plan that covers all employees. Benefits paid from the plan are based on years of service and average compensation during the five years immediately preceding retirement. The plan is fully funded. The firm contributed approximately $500,000 to the plan in the current reporting year.

  [For a defined contribution plan] The partnership operates a defined contribution plan that covers all employees who have been with the firm on a full-time basis for at least one year, except for partners. Partners are not included in the plan, because any payments made to their accounts would be considered distributions. Contributions made to this plan are based on a percentage of employee gross pay, with a cap of $9,000 per person, per year. The firm contributed approximately $210,000 to the plan in the current reporting year.

  The disclosures associated with retirement plans can be subject to a certain amount of debate, since many law firms do not disclose any retirement plan liability in their financial statements, under their interpretation of modified cash basis accounting. This does not mean that the liability does not exist, only that it is not being reported. Consequently, it can make sense to include a substantial footnote on the topic, even if no liability is included on the face of the financial statements.

- *Assets in escrow.* There may be cases in which a law firm acts as the custodian for assets belonging to its clients, such as cash or property. Since these assets do not belong to the firm, they do not appear in its financial statements. Nonetheless, their existence can be disclosed in the footnotes. The disclosure should note the aggregate amount held and state that these assets are not included in the financial statements. For example:

  As of the end of the reporting period, the partnership held approximately $1,000,000 of property on behalf of its clients. These assets are not included in the attached financial statements.

The exact contents of these disclosures will vary, depending on ongoing changes to the accounting standards that govern the disclosure of financial information, so the

---

[1] A defined benefit plan states the benefits that plan participants will receive. This puts the risk of changing benefit costs on the law firm.

[2] A defined contribution plan states the amount of money that the law firm will contribute to the plan. This puts the risk of changing benefit costs on plan participants.

preceding examples should only be considered baseline disclosures that will likely require additional text.

Notes are usually attached to financial statements that are being supplied to parties outside the firm, and only rarely to financial statements that are distributed just for internal use.

Accompanying Schedules

In addition to a set of notes, the financial statements may also include a set of schedules that expand upon various line items within the financial statements. These schedules are added when it appears that users of the financial statements need additional clarity on some topics. Examples of these schedules are:

- Detailed investment schedule
- Detailed receivables schedule
- Details of occupancy expenses
- Details regarding the various classifications of fixed assets
- Changes in individual partner accounts

Summary

The differentiating issue for the financial statements of law firms is their use of the modified cash basis of accounting. When this is the case, a firm may choose to exclude several items from its financial statements. Since there is no accounting standard that defines what should (or should not) be included in modified cash basis financial statements, it can be difficult to compare the financial statements of law firms. When the partners make choices about what to include in financial statements, they should at least commit to maintain the same report inclusions for as long as possible, so that the financial statements are consistent over a number of years.

Chapter 3
Law Firm Management Reporting

Introduction

The discussion in the preceding Law Firm Financial Statements chapter focused on the presentation of financial statements. However, partners need more specific information to effectively run a law firm. Consequently, there should be a series of weekly or monthly internal reports that are solely intended for their consumption, and which are intended to spotlight potential problems and opportunities. Examples of the information that may be contained within these reports are:

- Bad debts
- Billing rates
- Budget versus actual results
- Cash collected | overdue receivables
- Cash position
- Chargeable hours
- Clients lost
- Compensation costs
- Fee revenue
- Forecasted results
- Lawyer leverage
- Matter reporting
- New clients gained
- Profitability
- Realization rate
- Speed of billings
- Unbilled hours

Where possible, these reports should be presented on a trend line, so that unusual divergences from the long-run trend are immediately obvious.

This information should be compiled and presented in a consistent manner, which calls for the use of procedures that describe how information is to be collected and summarized for each item. Otherwise, inconsistently presented or inaccurate reports could trigger unnecessary partner investigations. We deal with these management reports in more detail in the following sections, along with several related topics.

Bad Debts

When a client refuses to pay for a billing, the resulting loss is a direct deduction from the profits of the firm, and therefore represents a reduction in the eventual amount of distributions to partners. A bad debts report should focus on which billings have the potential for becoming bad debts, while also noting any indicators of past payment problems that would indicate a higher risk of nonpayment. The following sample report shows those unpaid billings that are more than 90 days old, while also stating the aggregate and percentage amount of bad debts experienced with the indicated clients in prior periods. A significant experience with bad debts in the past should certainly put the focus on the indicated unpaid billings, while also raising the question of why the firm is continuing to do business with a client.

Sample Bad Debts Report

Client Name	Amount > 90 Days Old	Client Aggregate Bad Debts $	Client Aggregate Bad Debts %	Partner
Barnett Holdings	$12,000	$42,000	8%	Dixon
Eckstein Farms	5,000	500	1%	Bertrand
Galway Orchards	3,500	1,200	1%	Bertrand
Hayward Partners	7,200	4,100	2%	Dixon
Myers Investments	43,000	217,000	16%	Crane
O'Neill Manufacturing	10,000	--	--	Nichols

Based on the information provided in the preceding sample report, the history of non-payment for Barnett Holdings and Myers Investments is quite negative, which greatly raises the probability of nonpayment for both clients.

Billing Rates

Everyone in a law firm should be aware of the standard billing rate that applies to each position. What is less well-known is the actual billing rate that is applied to each client, or with which each individual is associated. For example, an associate may have a standard billing rate of $300/hour, but finds that she must routinely bill a $250/hour rate with several of her clients, who are too small to afford her full hourly rate. This actual billing rate can be discerned across a range of clients by dividing actual billings per person in a reporting period by their chargeable hours in that period. For example:

$40,160 total month's billing ÷ 160 hours billed = $251/hour actual billing rate

The reported $251/hour just calculated may seem fine, until one realizes that the person's standard billing rate is $400/hour. Thus, it can be useful to run a comparison of a person's actual billing rate to his or her standard rate, along with a variance. This analysis may be indicative of the unwillingness of clients to pay full rates, or perhaps the attorney is so inefficient that she finds it necessary to discount the prices being charged.

Budget versus Actual Results

The actual results of a law firm can be compared to its budget, both for the past month and for the year-to-date. This approach works best when the budget has been carefully constructed from realistic assumptions, so that it forms the basis for a reasonable comparison to actual results. When the budget is instead treated as a stretch goal that is unlikely to be achieved, there is little point in comparing it to actual results, since there will likely be wide disparities between the two sets of data. A sample budget versus actual report follows.

Sample Budget versus Actual Comparison Report

	Current Month		Year-to-Date	
	Actual	Budget	Actual	Budget
Professional fees	$1,000,000	$980,000	$5,430,000	$5,320,000
Employee compensation	512,000	518,000	2,635,000	2,640,000
Occupancy costs	35,000	35,000	165,000	163,000
Office expenses	18,000	14,000	83,000	74,000
Professional activities	28,000	10,000	109,000	103,000
General business expenses	14,000	13,000	71,000	69,000
Net profit	$393,000	$390,000	$2,367,000	$2,271,000

Cash Collected | Overdue Receivables

It can be useful to track the amount of cash collected, usually by responsible partner, and also identify the client that made the payment. This approach works best for smaller firms, where the cash position is highly dependent on a small number of cash receipts. In a larger firm, there may be so many cash receipts each day that an itemization by client will result in an excessively large report. A sample of this report appears in the following exhibit.

Sample Cash Collections Report

Partner	Client	Cash Collected
Amundsen, A.	Bright Lights Productions	$53,000
Amundsen, A.	Crystal Clear Optics	14,000
Amundsen, A.	Dental Partners LLC	29,000
Brighton, J.	Minnow Realty	81,000
Brighton, J.	Underhill Meatpacking	35,000
Month-to-date collections		$212,000
Month's cash collection goal		$600,000

An alternative approach is to focus on the amount of unpaid billings remaining outstanding. This unpaid billings aging report can be structured by responsible partner, so that each partner is made aware of the uncollected amounts of cash for which they are responsible, as well as the age of the receivables. A sample format appears in the following exhibit.

Sample Unpaid Billings Report

Partner	Total Overdue	0-30 Days	31-60 Days	61-90 Days	90+ Days
Davidson, M.	$1,560,000	$1,248,000	$203,000	$60,000	$49,000
Gentry, B.	828,000	662,000	108,000	40,000	18,000
Leavitt, S.	3,412,000	2,730,000	444,000	190,000	48,000
	$5,800,000	$4,640,000	$755,000	$290,000	$115,000

A more detailed report could be appended to the preceding unpaid billings report, specifying the exact invoices that have not been paid; the partners need this information in order to make collection calls to clients.

Cash Position

The amount of cash on hand is of particular importance when it is time to distribute earnings to partners. Consequently, the cash position report is one of the most closely-perused documents in a law firm as year-end approaches. The point of this report is not just to highlight the amount of cash on hand right now, but also the potential sources of collectible cash. The simplest reporting format is to state the current cash balance, subtract expected cash payments through year-end, and add in the total outstanding amount of billings receivable, which comes from the unpaid billings aging report. The partners can then use the detail on the aging report as their source document for contacting clients about obtaining payment. Thus, the quite brief format of the cash position report is:

+	Current cash position
-	Expected cash payments
+	Unpaid billings
=	Maximum potential year-end cash position

To introduce a dose of reality to the calculation, it may make sense to subtract expected bad debts from the unpaid billings line item, thereby reducing the calculated maximum potential year-end cash position.

Chargeable Hours

The core profit driver of a law firm is the number of chargeable hours accumulated by its personnel. Chargeable hours are those hours directly related to client engagements. Anyone in the organization can report chargeable hours, ranging from partners down to the administrative staff. A common management report is to accumulate the hours worked by each classification of employee within the firm and divide by the number of full-time equivalents within each classification to arrive at the average chargeable hours by classification. A sample report format follows.

Sample Chargeable Hours Report

	Senior Partners	Junior Partners	Associates	Paralegals
Total chargeable hours	20,640	10,140	63,040	7,000
Number of employees	12	6	32	10
Ave. chargeable hours	1,720	1,690	1,970	700
Last year average	1,700	1,740	1,850	820

The addition of the "last year average" to the preceding report provides a historical comparison. In the exhibit, there is a clear decline in the average number of chargeable hours for paralegals from the prior year, which may indicate the need for a layoff.

Chargeable hours should certainly be broken down by individual employee, since this can show under-utilization at the most fine-grained level within the firm. Chargeable hours reported by employee on a trend line is especially useful, since it can spotlight individuals who have proven difficult to work with or are inefficient, and who are therefore not assigned client work. Another variation appears in the following exhibit, where each person is given a monthly chargeable hours target, against which their actual reported chargeable hours are compared.

Sample Chargeable Hours Report Against Targeted Hours

	Current Month Hours			Year-to-Date Hours		
	Chargeable	Target	Variance	Chargeable	Target	Variance
Anderson, M.	120	140	-20	1,180	1,400	-220
Bellows, F.	160	150	+10	1,505	1,500	+5
Charnley, S.	30	120	-90	940	1,200	-360
Davis, E.	152	145	+7	1,400	1,450	-50
Foster, G.	139	145	-6	1,510	1,450	+60

Chargeable hours can also be aggregated by practice group. When combined with average billing rates, this reporting can be useful for discerning those practice areas that generate the most and least revenue, and which can therefore point toward those practice groups that should receive more (or fewer) resources.

Clients Lost

When the proportion of billings associated with departed clients exceeds the proportion of billings linked to new clients, a firm will find itself in a state of revenue decline. Consequently, it makes sense to keep track of which clients have not engaged in any billable activities with the firm within the past 12 months. This list should be linked to the name of the responsible partner, to clarify who should contact the departed client to renew relations. It can also be useful to state in the report the lifetime billings generated with these clients, which can be useful for highlighting which lost clients are the most important. A sample report presentation follows.

Sample Lost Clients Report

Client Name	Responsible Partner	Lifetime Billings
Addison Winery	Norris, Aaron	$1,089,000
Delta Farms Cooperative	Chapman, Henry	203,000
Full Quiver Farm	Jenkins, Lisa	129,000
Iron Horse Acquisitions	Atkinson, Paul	6,005,000
Long Run Music	Fletcher, Rose	52,000
		$7,478,000

In some cases, clients are lost at the initiative of the law firm, possibly due to the difficulty of the relationship, or perhaps because client pressure to keep fees low is adversely impacting the firm's realization rate.

Compensation Costs

The bulk of all law firm expenses are associated with compensation, so it makes sense to cluster all compensation-related expenses and operational information into a single report. This report can average compensation by employee classification, as well as headcount, and compare it to budgeted levels. The report is intended to spotlight anomalies that can be corrected by adjusting headcount and compensation levels. A sample report follows.

Sample Compensation Report

	Actual	Budget
Average compensation:		
Associates	$182,000	$180,000
Paralegals	65,000	64,000
Secretaries	52,000	53,000
Other administrative	41,000	40,000
Headcount:		
Partners	80	82
Associates	209	205
Paralegals	42	41
Secretaries	63	62
Other administrative	29	32
Ratio of staff to lawyers:		
Paralegals	0.15	0.14
Secretaries	0.22	0.22
Other administrative	0.10	0.11

The ratio of staff to lawyers in the preceding report can be compared to local benchmarks, as well as plotted on a trend line, to see if the firm's staffing levels are unusually high or low.

Fee Revenue

The partners should have a firm idea of which clients bring in the most revenue. Consequently, a client list, sorted in declining order by fee revenue, can be useful for understanding which clients are the most important. This can be useful for deciding which clients deserve the highest levels of client service, which usually translates into a high volume of available staff time and the most rapid responses to requests made. To improve the accuracy of this report, it can make sense to subtract out bad debts and perhaps any billings that have been unpaid for a protracted period of time. A sample report appears next.

Sample Fee Revenue Report

Client Name	Fee Revenue	Partner
Medusa Medical	$3,178,000	Nance
New Centurion Corp.	2,408,000	Harwell
Electronic Inference Corp.	1,947,000	Williams
Nova Corporation	1,430,000	Nance
Radiosonde Communications	1,260,000	Harwell
Twill Machinery	937,000	Williams
Henderson Industrial	802,000	Duncan
Viking Fitness	707,000	Duncan
Quest Clothiers	682,000	Nance

Forecasted Results

It can be exceedingly difficult to forecast the results of a law firm through the end of the year, for several reasons. First, it is usually quite difficult to forecast with any accuracy for more than a few months into the future. Second, a higher level of forecasting precision requires a more detailed forecast, which results in a cost-benefit tradeoff of improved precision at the cost of more forecasting effort. And third, revenue forecasts come from partners, who may consider this to be too much administrative effort when they could instead be engaged in billable work. Consequently, we suggest using a relatively streamlined forecasting report that mixes detailed revenue estimating for the most significant clients with summary-level estimates for most other parts of the business. In the following sample forecast report, note the presence of a separate line item for new hires | layoffs that represents a rough guess at staffing changes that coincide with forecasted changes in revenue levels through the end of the year. Also, note the use of projections by quarter instead of by month, which reduces the forecasting effort.

Sample Forecast

	Year-to-Date	Quarter 2	Quarter 3	Quarter 4	Total Projected
Fee revenue:					
Celsius Corporation	$182,000	$175,000	$165,000	$160,000	$682,000
Argyle Clothes	140,000	180,000	100,000	80,000	500,000
Smith Industrial	129,000	125,000	125,000	125,000	504,000
Currency Bank	107,000	100,000	150,000	150,000	507,000
Giro Cabinetry	100,000	85,000	--	--	185,000
All other clients	432,000	500,000	600,000	700,000	2,232,000
Total fee revenue	1,090,000	1,165,000	1,140,000	1,215,000	4,610,000
Compensation expense	600,000	600,000	600,000	600,000	2,400,000
General office expense	120,000	130,000	130,000	145,000	525,000
New hires	layoffs	--	--	--	150,000	150,000
Forecasted profit	$370,000	$435,000	$410,000	$320,000	$1,535,000

Lawyer Leverage

In a law firm, leverage refers to the ratio of equity partners to all other lawyers in the firm. When there is a high leverage ratio, this indicates that the distributable income of the equity partners should increase, since they are benefiting from the profits generated by everyone else in the firm. This concept only works when the non-partner personnel are sufficiently highly utilized to generate enough fee income to cover their direct costs. The leverage ratio is:

Number of equity partners ÷ Number of all other lawyers = Lawyer leverage ratio

Matter Reporting

It can be useful to report on the current status of all matters being handled by the firm, especially those that are being handled on a fixed fee basis. When there is a fixed fee, the partners will want to closely oversee the number of hours and other monetary commitments being charged to a matter, and compare total accumulated costs to the budgeted amount. An essential element of this report is an estimate of billings as a percentage of the budget, in order to spot any matters on which the firm appears to be going over its budget. A sample report follows.

Sample Report of Matter Status

Client	Matter	Total Unbilled Time	Total Fees Billed to Date	Budget	Fees Billed as Percent of Budget	Fees Billed and Unbilled Time as Percent of Budget
Allison Bros.	Tax strategy	$20,000	$61,000	$100,000	61%	81%
Artemis	Property seizure	4,000	8,000	50,000	16%	24%
Attitude Inc.	Product recall	31,000	94,000	200,000	47%	63%
AZ Clothiers	Lawsuit appeal	8,000	34,000	60,000	57%	70%
Bristle Inc.	Investor filing	11,000	18,000	30,000	60%	97%
Bubbles Co.	Acquisition	42,000	290,000	325,000	89%	102%

New Clients Gained

The ongoing addition of new clients is critical to the financial health of a law firm, but it can be difficult to generate a report that conveys meaningful information about a client for which no work has yet been done. One possibility is to delay any reporting on them until a modest period of time has passed, such as three months, and then issue a report that shows the amount of billed and unbilled time for each of them. Doing so conveys some sense of the size of the client's potential business. This approach could be followed for the first year with a new client, after which it is pulled from the report and categorized with more established clients. A sample report follows.

Sample New Clients Report

Client Name	Practice Group	Partner	Billed and Unbilled Hours			
			Quarter 1	Quarter 2	Quarter 3	Quarter 4
Best Imports	Tax Law	Morrison	$--	$--	$13,000	$14,000
Carter Designs	Patent Law	Boyd	--	15,000	12,000	4,000
Douglas Cakes	Franchise	Saito	2,000	--	3,000	--
Glitter Estates	Bankruptcy	Pierce	32,000	47,000	--	--
Lehman Constr.	Construction	Christiansen	7,000	6,000	10,000	3,000
Pinto Architects	Franchise	Miller	4,000	9,000	8,000	5,000
Totals			$45,000	$77,000	$46,000	$26,000

Profitability

The overall profitability of a law firm is presented in its financial statements. But what if the firm wants to calculate its profitability for individual offices or practice groups? If so, it will need to record revenue and expense transactions using the expanded charge codes discussed in Chapter 1, The Essentials of Law Firm Accounting. By doing so, the accounting software should be configurable to present segmented profits in the manner that appears in the next exhibit.

Sample Profitability Report by Office

	Boston	Charleston	Dallas	Denver
Professional fees	$2,700,000	$2,100,000	$4,600,000	$1,900,000
Expenses	-2,400,000	-1,620,000	-3,400,000	-1,380,000
Net profits	$300,000	$480,000	$1,200,000	$520,000

The expenses in the report can be expanded into a larger number of more-detailed line items, though this is only recommended when the extra level of detail will result in actionable items. Otherwise, excessive detail merely obscures the main point of the report, which is profitability by office.

The same reporting format can be prepared for practice areas, since the report may reveal that certain practice groups are yielding unsatisfactory performance, which may result in the strategic decision to close down certain groups and concentrate the firm's efforts in those areas where greater profits can be obtained.

A potential problem with the preceding report is the inherent assumption that all expenses can be traced directly to an office, practice area, or client. In reality, many law firm costs are part of its overhead, such as office rent and utilities. These overhead costs can be pooled together and then allocated out in various ways, depending on the nature of the report. If these allocated costs are a substantial part of the cost structure of the firm, it may make sense to report them separately from direct (traceable) expenses. This concept appears in the following exhibit, where the profitability report is structured for practice groups.

Sample Profitability Report by Practice Group

	Arbitration	Family Law	Labor Law	Personal Injury
Professional fees	$4,200,000	$1,800,000	$800,000	$5,050,000
Direct expenses	-1,800,000	-920,000	-480,000	-710,000
Indirect expenses	-1,700,000	-680,000	-270,000	-2,240,000
Net profits	$700,000	$200,000	$50,000	$2,100,000

It can be especially interesting to apply this report format to individual clients, since it may uncover instances in which losses or substandard profits are being generated, which may lead to the termination of relations with a few clients. These situations tend to be confined to a relatively small number of clients, typically those that have refused to pay the firm, resulting in significant bad debt write-offs. The report may also reveal clients that have imposed so much pricing pressure on the firm that its fees are lower than its costs. A report similar to the following exhibit is useful for highlighting these problem clients. The exhibit only shows unprofitable clients, but could also be designed to report profits for *all* clients, in order to spotlight which ones are most worthy of the highest level of service.

Sample Profitability Report by Client

Client Name	Fee Revenue	Direct Costs	Bad Debts	Net Loss
Behemoth Medical	$41,000	$43,000	$--	-$2,000
Bland Cabinets	13,000	7,000	13,000	-7,000
Cud Farms	27,000	16,000	12,000	-1,000
Horton Corporation	52,000	40,000	15,000	-3,000
Monk Books	86,000	53,000	46,000	-13,000

Realization Rate

The realization rate is the proportion of billable hours at standard billing rates that is actually billed to clients. This rate can be broken down by employee classification, since junior employees tend to be less efficient, resulting in fewer of their billable hours being billed to clients. A low realization rate may also be triggered by client pressure to keep rates low, or due to a misunderstanding regarding the scope of the work to be performed. A sample report format follows.

Sample Realization Rate Report

	Senior Partners	Junior Partners	Associates	Paralegals
Standard fees generated	$2,417,000	$3,084,000	$6,277,000	$420,000
Actual fees billed	2,345,000	2,930,000	5,603,000	410,000
Realization rate	97%	95%	89%	98%

Realization rates can also be aggregated by partner, office, and practice group.

Speed of Billings

A law firm may have a substantial amount of its working capital tied up in either uncollected fees receivable or unbilled time charges. There are several reasons for this large investment. First, partners are reluctant to issue billings until a matter has been completed, which can be an issue when it may take several months to bring a matter to a resolution. And second, once unbilled time charges are converted into a billing, any under-realization of time charges will become apparent, which may focus unwanted attention on the under-realized amount. Nonetheless, there should be a strong focus on issuing billings on a relatively speedy basis, if only to improve the cash position of the firm.

The speed of billings can be expressed by calculating the proportion of the combined amount of uncollected fees receivable and unbilled time charges to the monthly average time charges compiled by a firm. The following table illustrates the calculation.

Sample Speed of Billings Calculation

+	Uncollected fees receivable	$2,350,000
+	Unbilled time charges	1,850,000
=	Investment in client services	$4,200,000
÷	Monthly average time charges	$1,400,000
=	Speed of billings and collections	3.0 months

In the sample table, it takes 3.0 months from the point at which a law firm creates a time charge until the date when the related cash payment from a client is eventually received.

This report might be examined by the partners with increasing frequency towards the end of the fiscal year, since they have a strong interest in collecting cash, which is then distributed to them as their share of the firm's income.

Unbilled Hours

The partners should have some insight into the nature of unbilled hours, since some portion of these hours will eventually be written off, while others may not be included in a client billing for months. One way to present this information is to create an unbilled fees aging schedule, which sorts the unbilled hours into time buckets. A sample format appears in the following schedule, where the same information is presented for the preceding two years, in order to give a basis of comparison.

Sample Unbilled Hours Aging Schedule

Time Bucket	As of Today	One Year Prior	Two Years Prior
Last 3 months	$3,750,000	$3,620,000	$3,510,000
3+ months to 6 months	750,000	725,000	700,000
6+ months to 9 months	375,000	360,000	350,000
9+ months	180,000	160,000	140,000
Less: Write-offs reserve	-425,000	-415,000	-400,000
Net value of unbilled hours	$4,630,000	$4,450,000	$4,300,000

To gain even greater clarity about the sources of unbilled hours, the preceding schedule could be further refined to show just the hours for a specific practice group or employee.

Attorney-Specific Reporting

The ultimate revenue generator for a law firm is its attorneys, so it can make sense to prepare a standardized performance report for each one. This report can then be used by partners to follow up with each attorney in regard to their goals. The following report shows a possible report format for the more essential performance indicators.

Sample Performance Indicators by Attorney

March Results	Attorney Names				
	Anderson	Carter	Denton	Ibrahim	Poor
Utilization	92%	110%	**51%**	89%	87%
Billings	$44,000	$48,000	**$22,000**	$43,000	$38,000
Collections	$39,000	**$9,000**	$20,000	$39,000	**$19,000**
New client billings	$4,200	$1,000	$6,000	**$500**	**$250**
Pro bono hours	10	8	**25**	6	5

In the preceding report, unusually high or low results are stated in bold, which draws the attention of the reader to them. This is a form of exception reporting, which is noted further in the following section.

Exception Reports

If a law firm were to issue all of the reports described in this chapter, it could end up issuing quite a hefty reporting package to its partners. However, partners have other concerns, such as maintaining revenues, and so will not have time to examine the reports in detail. To narrow their focus to just those issues that are most critical to the firm, the accountant can sort through the various reports, select just those issues that are not meeting expectations, and aggregate these items into an exception report, along with an explanation of each reported item. This means that the contents of the exception report will vary continually, as issues percolate up the criticality list, are dealt with, and then vanish from the report. Examples of items that might appear on this report are:

- Unusually low billable hours reported by specific attorneys
- Unusually old unpaid billings
- The imminent projected decline in the firm's cash balance below a predetermined minimum threshold

An exception report is intended to focus the attention of partners, so an ideal length is just one page, with perhaps five topics addressed in the report. The report should also state who is dealing with each issue, so that partners can contact the responsible party for further information.

> **Tip:** Consider creating an exception report for each practice area, so that the essential performance issues can be delivered to the partner(s) in charge of each practice area on a regular basis.

Operating and Financial Metrics

The bulk of the discussion thus far has been on the development of reports that can be used to assist in the management of a law firm. In addition, the firm should develop a standard set of operating and financial metrics, of which the following are the most common:

- *Average billed rate per person.* This is total fee billings divided by the number of hours billed. This information is typically calculated by position, such as partner, associate, and paralegal. It can be compared to regional billing rates to see if the firm needs to adjust its standard rates charged.
- *Average fee per client.* This is the total amount billed in the period, divided by the number of clients billed. This metric should be tracked on a trend line, to track changes in the average fee over time. This figure is impacted by on-going changes in the hourly billing rate.
- *Billable hours per person.* This is the total number of billable hours worked, divided by the number of full-time equivalents[3]. This metric is useful for spotting an overabundance of staff in relation to the amount of available work, which could lead to a layoff.
- *Billing realization percentage.* This is the aggregate amount of client billings generated in comparison to the aggregate amount of billable hours accumulated. Any amount less than 100% billing realization indicates that the firm has chosen to write off some portion of billable hours prior to issuing billings.
- *Charge-off percentage.* This is the aggregate amount of billings written off, divided by total billings. This information is used to determine the proportion of billings that are never collected, and is especially useful when tracked on a trend line, to spot long-term changes in the ability of clients to pay.
- *Client retention.* This is the ratio of the number of clients billed in the past 12 months to the same clients who were billed in the preceding 12 months. This metric shows the firm's efficiency and quality of service in retaining customers, though an excessively high ratio can indicate that the firm is not spending enough money and effort on attracting new clients.
- *Days of fees receivable.* This is the fee portion of unpaid billings divided by annual revenues, and then multiplied by the number of days in the year. The intent is to determine the average number of days required to collect fees from clients.
- *Dormant client percentage.* This is the proportion of clients for which the firm has not handled a matter in the past two or three years. This metric can reveal an opportunity, since it is less difficult to make inquiries with these clients for additional work than pursuing entirely new clients. A high dormant client percentage can also be an indicator that clients have been dissatisfied with prior work, and so no longer contact the firm.
- *Effective hourly rate.* This is the total amount received from clients divided by the hours worked on behalf of those clients. This metric can be applied to practice groups or to individual clients. A low realization rate can drop the effective hourly rate.

---

[3] One full-time equivalent equals one employee working full-time.

- *Information technology as percentage of revenue.* This is the amount of money spent on information technology (such as software, hardware, networks, and mobile devices), divided by revenues. The resulting percentage can then be compared to benchmark figures for similar firms within the same region.
- *Marketing expenditure as percentage of revenue.* This is the amount of money spent on marketing activities, divided by revenues. The resulting percentage can then be compared to benchmark figures for similar firms within the same region.
- *Number of matters per client.* This is the ratio of the number of matters billed to the number of clients billed. A high ratio indicates that the firm is doing a good job of being a full-service provider for its existing clients, maximizing billings to each one.
- *Percent of revenue from new clients.* This is the proportion of revenue generated from new clients (starting within the past 12 months) to all revenues generated within the past 12 months. This information can be tracked on a trend line to judge the firm's success in locating new clients.
- *Ratio of associates to partners.* As the title states, this is the proportion of full-time equivalent associates to partners. A high ratio typically equates to more partner profits, since profits earned by associates will flow through to partner distributions.

A possible concern when reporting these metrics is that most of them will change only a small amount (if at all) from period to period. When there is no appreciable movement in a metric, it can make sense to not report it, thereby focusing attention on the much smaller number of metrics that are showing some variability. The full set of metrics could be issued on a quarterly or annual basis.

Summary

Management reporting is an essential requirement for a law firm that wants to generate solid financial returns over the long term. This does not mean that the partners can simply assemble a few relevant reports, arrange for them to be distributed once a month, and then return to their ongoing billable work. Instead, the contents of these reports must be constantly tweaked to ensure that they contain the most relevant information that pertains to the firm's current situation, as well as where it expects to be over the next few years. In addition, these reports must be delivered to those individuals within the firm who are in the best position to take advantage of the information, and as frequently as needed – which may be on a daily, weekly, monthly, or quarterly basis. A final point regarding management reports is that certain information will not be needed forever – at some point, the recipients need to decide whether the provided information is still useful to them. If not, it is best to remove this information from the reports, so that the report recipients can spend more time focusing on just those metrics that are most relevant to them at the moment. For example, a law firm decides to create a new practice group, and decides to place a reporting focus on its revenue, expenses, and profitability for the first year, until it can be proven that the group is capable of meeting the firm's performance standards.

Chapter 4
Law Firm Controls

Introduction

A law firm is a service business, and so has relatively few assets to protect. Instead, its main risk is through the loss of funds in the billing process, either because hours worked are not billed, or because the amounts billed are not collected. In addition, it must ensure that financial transactions are correctly recorded and aggregated into the financial statements. A well-designed system of controls can minimize the risk of problems in these areas. This chapter covers the main touchpoints within a law firm that should be addressed with a system of controls.

Control Cost-Benefit

The imposition of a new control is not usually greeted by employees with cries of joy. The problem is that each additional control adds more administrative time, thereby reducing the amount of time available to work on client matters. Therefore, when developing a system of controls, it is highly useful to look at each control from the perspectives of both incremental risk reduction and incremental costs added. In many cases, it will make sense to avoid a control entirely, or at least weaken it, if the payoff is a significant improvement in the time available for billable work. This cost-benefit principle is especially important in cases where controls impact people who generate substantial amounts of revenue, such as partners and senior associates.

Control Issues Specific to Law Firms

The essential control problem with law firms is that they are not organizationally designed to have strong controls. Instead, the focus is largely on client relations, researching matters on behalf of clients, and monitoring billable hours. In other words, the focus of a law firm is on the generation of revenue – it is *not* on the monitoring of expenses. A partner is usually designated as being responsible for all administrative activities of the firm, of which accounting is a part. However, an administrative partner is not trained in controls, and so will probably only install them as a reaction to losses that have already occurred.

As a law firm grows and its operations become more complex, it will need a more specialized person to take responsibility for controls, perhaps a chief administrative officer, chief financial officer, or controller. This person either understands control systems or can bring in specialists to examine the firm's systems and make recommendations regarding the system of controls.

The control environment worsens when a firm opens multiple offices, since responsibility is now diffused across a broad geographic region. In this case, the organizational structure will need to expand, encompassing dedicated accountants at each location that use a standardized accounting system and controls. In this environment, it is useful to have an internal audit team that can examine controls and accounting procedures across the organization, noting areas in which improvements are needed. The internal audit manager should report to the management committee of the firm, in order to avoid being influenced by managers in local offices.

Billing and Cash Receipt Controls

The accumulation and billing of hours to clients, as well as the proper reimbursement of expenditures made on behalf of clients, represents the largest cluster of cash flows in a law firm, and therefore the area most in need of controls. Controls begin with the accumulation of hours worked, and can include the following:

- *Mandate daily timekeeping.* This control is a policy requirement, that everyone enter their hours worked into the central timekeeping system on a daily basis. Doing so corrects the inevitable problem of someone not remembering what hours were worked during an earlier day, nor the nature of the tasks performed, which leads to incorrect client billings and incorrect descriptions of work performed. In addition, promptly-recorded time records allows for faster month-end billings to clients, which in turn enhances the speed with which clients pay the firm. It can make sense to place an administrative person in charge of examining time records every day and following up with any parties that have not entered the required information.
- *Institute automated reviews.* Many timekeeping software packages contain automated error checks that can be useful for spotting information that has been entered incorrectly. These reviews are especially useful because there is no staff labor involved. For example, the system can flag an excessive number of hours being charged (such as 26 hours in a day). Or, it can flag instances in which fewer than eight hours were logged in a day, which can uncover billable time that was not recorded. The system can also be set up to only allow an employee access to specific client charge codes, thereby keeping them from inadvertently (or deliberately) charging time to clients with which they are not associated.
- *Proof the billing.* The individually-recorded billing hours for each person need to be accurately transferred into the formal client billing. To ensure that this information is compiled correctly, have a second person proof each preliminary billing, checking to see if all billable hours were correctly transferred to the billing and that the correct billing rates were used.
- *Approve the billing.* A partner should review and formally approve every billing. This is not only to include another accuracy check in the billing process; in addition, the partner needs to decide the amount that will be charged, which may result in an under- or over-realization. In addition, the partner is the first point of contact with the client, and so must be familiar with the billing in case the client calls about it.

- *Review unbilled fees.* Unbilled fees tend to be reviewed in less detail than billable hours that are being included in a client billing. Consequently, it can make sense to periodically examine unbilled fees to see if any have been incorrectly coded and can be included in a billing. It can be especially useful to sort the unbilled fees by age, so that the oldest unbilled amounts can be examined in more detail.

- *Separate billing and cash recordation activities.* The person responsible for preparing billings should not participate in the recordation of incoming client payments. Otherwise, the person could alter the amounts billed to clients in order to hide the theft of incoming cash from the firm.

- *Issue monthly statements.* Issue a statement to all clients if they have any balances outstanding at the end of each month. Doing so can highlight cases in which billings were not sent or were lost in transit. The contact information listed on these statements should not be the billing clerk. If the billing clerk is engaged in fraud, it hardly helps to route client inquiries straight back to that person.

- *Separate cash collection duties.* Someone other than the firm's cashier should open the mail each day and make a list of all client checks received. This list is created and stored in the mailroom, and acts as a check on the activities of the cashier, who might otherwise be tempted to remove checks or cash prior to logging these payments into the accounting system. In addition, two mailroom people should open the mail and log client payments, thereby minimizing the risk of theft in the mailroom. Finally, someone should routinely compare the mailroom's list of checks received to the bank deposit slip for each day. If the deposit slip's total is lower than the mailroom total, the cashier may have stolen some client payments.

- *Conduct daily bank reconciliations.* It can be quite useful to conduct a daily bank reconciliation by accessing the bank's latest updates to the firm's account information and tracing it back to internal cash account records. Doing so gives the firm early notice of any client checks that have been rejected due to insufficient funds, as well as providing an opportunity to spot questionable checks clearing the bank.

- *Send to a lockbox.* Have clients send their payments directly to a bank lockbox, so that no payments are ever handled on the premises. Instead, the bank receives all payments, for which the cashier can access an electronic image on the bank's website for accounting purposes.

- *Approve all significant write-offs.* The cashier may steal a client payment and then cover his tracks by writing off the amount stolen, as though the client never paid it. This issue can be addressed by requiring partner approval of all write-offs that exceed a certain minimum amount. A variation is to periodically review a trend line of monthly write-offs. A spike in this trend or a gradually increasing amount of write-offs can indicate that someone is manipulating the write-offs.

Payroll Controls

The largest cluster of cash outflows in a law firm is usually the compensation paid to its employees. In the following bullet points, we highlight those controls most necessary for the avoidance of losses linked to payroll:

- *Approve all pay changes.* Every pay rate change entered into the payroll system should be approved by an authorized person. Also, if the payroll system has a change log, monitor it to ensure that only authorized changes are being made to the system.
- *Approve the payroll register.* Once a preliminary version of the payroll is ready for processing, have an authorized person review the preliminary payroll register in detail and approve it before final payroll processing can commence. The intent is to spot and investigate any cases in which pay rates or hours worked appear to be incorrect.
- *Pay by direct deposit.* When the firm pays employees by direct deposit, there is no need to control checks on the premises; instead, money is transferred directly from the firm's bank account to the personal accounts of employees. This feature is most accessible when the payroll processing function is outsourced to a third party.
- *Separate payroll duties.* Have one person prepare the payroll, another authorize it, and another create payments, thereby reducing the risk of fraud unless multiple people collude in doing so. In smaller firms where there are not enough personnel for a proper separation of duties, at least insist on having someone review and authorize the payroll before payments are issued.

Additional controls related to cutting checks to employees are covered in the following section, Payables Controls.

A particular concern with payroll is the risk of having *ghost employees* – individuals who are being paid by the firm, but who do not work for it. Someone who prepares the payroll creates and maintains a ghost employee in the payroll system, and then intercepts and cashes the paychecks intended for this person. Preventing this fraud involves having all partners conduct a careful review of the payroll records for their direct reports to ensure that all employees are valid. A good way to detect ghost employees is to look for anyone who has few or no deductions from his or her pay. A perpetrator rarely goes to the trouble of creating a complete set of benefit enrollments, especially since doing so will reduce the amount of money that they can steal from the firm. Another detection technique is to look at the back of each deposited check to see if there are two endorsements. The first endorsement will be a forgery in the name of the ghost employee, while the second endorsement is the name of the employee cashing the check.

Payables Controls

A law firm will process a significant number of accounts payable transactions on an ongoing basis, which constitutes a major cash outflow that should be carefully controlled. In the following bullet points, we note the most essential and cost-effective controls to impose on the payables process:

- *Approve all expenditures*. Every proposed expenditure above a minimum threshold level should be approved by an authorized person. For example, an expense report should be approved by someone occupying a higher position within the firm, while a partner should approve the expense report of another partner. Supplier invoices should be approved by the partner responsible for administration of the office. Possible streamlining options are to pay for minor items without approval, using a company credit card, and to automatically approve recurring invoices, such as rent payments.

- *Split check printing and signing*. One person should prepare checks, and a different person should sign them. By doing so, there is a cross-check on the issuance of cash.

- *Store all checks in a locked location*. Unused check stock should always be stored in a locked location. Otherwise, checks can be stolen and fraudulently filled out and cashed. This means that any signature plates or stamps should also be stored in a locked location.

- *Track the sequence of check numbers used*. Maintain a log in which are listed the range of check numbers used during a check run. This is useful for determining if any checks in storage might be missing. This log should not be kept with the stored checks, since someone could steal the log at the same time they steal checks.

- *Approve payments*. A sufficiently senior individual within the firm should sign all checks, reviewing supporting documentation to ensure that each payment is valid. The same approach should be applied to the approval of wire transfers, possibly including a required call-back from the bank to verify all outbound wire transfers that exceed a certain dollar amount. It is especially important to have a robust approval process for wire transfers, since just a single unauthorized wire transfer could wipe out the balance in a firm's bank account.

- *Code for client reimbursed expenditures*. There should be a robust coding system in place that clearly identifies any payments being incurred on behalf of clients, since these items can be billed to the clients. This system can include ongoing training in how to code for these expenditures, as well as in-house audits of payables to spot reimbursable items that were incorrectly coded.

- *Audit recurring payments*. The payables system may be set up to continually issue the same payment amount to the same supplier on the same date of every month. To guard against paying these recurring amounts for an excessive period of time, conduct an occasional review of all recurring payments to verify that they should still be paid.

- *Mail all checks directly*. All signed checks should be sent straight to the mailroom for delivery to suppliers. Otherwise, someone within the firm could insert a fake supplier invoice into the system, cut a check, have it signed, and then extract the signed check and cash it.

- *Maintain separate accounts for client cash.* A firm may handle substantial amounts of cash on behalf of its clients. If so, these funds should not be commingled with the firm's own funds. Instead, there should be a separate bank account for each client's funds, for which all outbound cash transfers are tightly controlled, subject to partner approval.
- *Compare to budget.* If the firm has prepared a realistic budget on a monthly basis, it can make sense to run a budget versus actual report and review any of the larger variances that appear on the report. These variances will highlight unexpected expenses, either in terms of the size of an expense or its timing.

Partner-Related Controls

The partners have an obvious interest in the accuracy of their capital accounts, as well as in the calculations of the income distributable to them. The following controls can be used to minimize the risk of errors in partner accounts:

- *Audit accounts.* Conduct a periodic examination of the partner accounts, rolling forward account balances from the last time when an audit was conducted. The audit should verify all account changes, with particular emphasis on the accuracy of partner distributions. A potential concern to watch for is that partner transactions are being recorded in the wrong partner account.
- *Verify distribution calculations.* Once preliminary partner distribution calculations have been made, have a second person review them. This verification should include tracing the distribution terms in the partnership agreement to the distribution calculation, verifying the designation of each partner (such as junior, senior, or retired), verifying that all partners are included, and manually recalculating the distribution.

Summary

A core issue for smaller law firms is that there are not enough people on the premises to engage in a proper separation of duties. Instead, there may be just one person responsible for all accounting activities. When that is the case, at least involve a partner in the review and approval of key transactions, so that someone is (for example) approving billings, write-offs, and payroll registers. In a larger firm, the problem shifts to keeping control of a much more complex environment, where there are multiple offices and practice groups. In the latter case, the focus should be on having a dedicated accounting and internal auditing group that strives for full enforcement of a standardized set of controls across the organization.

Glossary

A

Accrual basis. The practice of recording revenue when it is earned and expenses when liabilities are incurred or assets consumed.

B

Business transaction. An economic event with a third party that is recorded in a firm's accounting system.

C

Capital account. An account used by partnerships to track the net investment balance of partners.

Capitalization limit. The amount paid for an asset, above which it is recorded as a fixed asset.

Cash basis. The practice of recording revenue when cash is received and recording expenses when cash is paid.

Contra account. An account that offsets the balance in another, related account with which it is paired.

D

Distributable income. The amount of net income that is available for distribution to active partners.

F

Financial statements. A collection of reports about a firm's financial results, financial position, and cash flows.

Fixed asset. A purchased item that has a life span of greater than one reporting period, and which exceeds the firm's capitalization limit.

G

General ledger. The master set of accounts that summarize all transactions occurring within a firm.

L

Lawyer leverage. The ratio of equity partners to all other lawyers in a firm.

O

Operating expense. Any expense associated with the general and administrative activities of a firm.

Over-realization. When a billing exceeds the standard billing rate.

P

Posting. The process of shifting the balance in a subsidiary ledger into the general ledger.

Practice group. A group of professionals working within a designated area of expertise.

Progress billing. An invoice for services completed to date.

R

Realization rate. The proportion of billable hours at standard billing rates that is actually billed to clients.

Retainer. A fee paid in advance in order to secure the services of a law firm.

S

Statement of cash flows. A financial report that presents the cash inflows and outflows experienced during a reporting period.

Statement of net assets. A financial report that aggregates a firm's assets and liabilities, as well as partners' equity.

Statement of revenues and expenses. A financial report that aggregates a firm's revenues and expenses, ending with a profit or loss.

U

Under-realization. When a billing is less than the standard billing rate.

Index

www.ingramcontent.com/pod-product-compliance
Lightning Source LLC
Chambersburg PA
CBHW051421200326
41520CB00023B/7322